THE GET-ALONGS
A GUIDE FOR TEACHING SOCIAL SKILLS

Written by
CAROL CUMMINGS, PH.D.

SOCIAL SKILL UNITS

LISTENING
GIVING PUT-UPS (COMPLIMENTS)
PROBLEM SOLVING
ANGER MANAGEMENT
SHARING
RECOGNIZING FEELINGS
TATTLING VS. REPORTING
MANNERS

MAY ALSO BE USED TO ACCOMPANY THE SOCIAL SKILL BOOKS:

Won't You Ever Listen?
Sticks & Stones
A Win-Win Day
I'm Always in Trouble
Sharing is Caring
Finding Feelings
Tattlin' Madeline
Copy the Cat

ABOUT THE AUTHOR

Dr. Cummings conducts workshops for parents and teachers throughout the world on motivation, social skills, reading and writing strategies, classroom management, cooperative learning, and teaching diverse classrooms. She works on a research project for at-risk children at the University of Washington (Raising Healthy Children) and teaches at Seattle Pacific University. Teachers in the research project, Raising Healthy Children, have contributed many of the ideas for these social skill units. Dr. Cummings is the author of 15 books for teachers and children.

ISBN 1-881660-02-8

©Teaching, Inc., 1993
Third printing, 1998
All rights reserved, including translation.
Printed in Taiwan

Teaching, Inc.
P.O. Box 788
Edmonds, WA 98020
(425) 774 0755

TABLE OF CONTENTS

INTRODUCTION

This is a manual of how-tos and tips for teaching social skills to children. As a staff developer working on several research projects through the University of Washington, I have had the opportunity to observe teachers using these techniques successfully to teach interpersonal skills. The research is very clear that children with prosocial behavior are more successful in school and have more friends. If you need more convincing about the necessity for teaching social skills, then read the rationale that follows!

RATIONALE

Have you heard teachers commenting that kids today aren't like they used to be? Have you asked yourself why? Think back to when you began school and try to answer these questions:

When you arrived home from school, did you have someone at home to greet you? Over 75% of today's children have no family member waiting to greet them after school.

What did you do after school? Did you do chores, homework, or go outside to play with friends? Children in the 90s are sitting down in front of the television set. In fact, they are averaging 28-30 hours a week in television viewing. Did you sit down to dinner at a table with family members present? What do most children today do?

Children today simply haven't had the same opportunities to learn and practice social skills that we had. Yet, since 1848 there has been a space on report cards to evaluate students on their use of social skills such as listening and sharing. While it probably wasn't necessary to teach these skills through direct instruction before, today it is!

Employers tell us that more employees lose their jobs because they lack social skills than because they lack technical skills. In 1991, the U.S. Department of Labor, in conjunction with U.S. employers, recommended the development of interpersonal skills as a goal for graduates from our school system. The SCANS report (Secretary's Commission on Achieving Necessary Skills) listed five competencies for the workplace:

- resources
- interpersonal skills
- information skills
- systems skills
- technology utilization skills

This curriculum guide is designed to teach *interpersonal* skills.

This guide provides activities to increase a student's emotional intelligence. Daniel Goleman (1995), in his book *Emotional Intelligence*, argues that a high IQ is not a major predictor of success in life; that emotional intelligence is a bigger predictor. He defines emotional intelligence as:

1. SELF-AWARENESS The awareness of our "gut feelings" is a prerequisite to being able to act on them or to change our mood. The unit in this manual, *Feelings*, provides many activities to help students recognize primary emotions and what causes them.

2. MOOD MANAGEMENT Socially competent individuals have control over their emotions—find a balance in their display of emotions. Goleman quotes Aristotle to emphasize the appropriateness of emotions:

> *Anyone can become angry—that is easy. But to be angry with the right person, to the right degree, at the right time, for the right purpose, and in the right way—this is not easy.*

The units on anger management and problem solving will help students develop "mood management."

In addition, the unit on problem solving will help students realize that they can choose what they think. Positive self-talk can influence our feelings. A person with a "win-win" attitude is likely to think of constructive ways to deal with their problems. A person with a "lose-lose" attitude becomes a blamer and thinks of ways to give up. The activities in the unit will help students focus on the consequences of the choices they make. Taking time to consider both the pros and cons of the options one has in solving a problem will minimize dysfunctional behavior.

One characteristic of at-risk learners is that they lack impulse control and have difficulty predicting the consequences of their actions. Socially competent individuals are able to delay gratification as they pursue their goals. Activities in the anger management, problem solving and tattling units will assist with impulse control.

3. **SELF-MOTIVATION** The attitude that one works hard to get smart characterizes successful individuals. Self-motivation is that enthusiasm to work hard. Many of the activities in this manual will help students see the relationship between their effort and their success. For example, teaching students to keep goal cards provides a concrete reminder that each small step they take places them closer to goal accomplishment.

4. **EMPATHY** This is the ability to know how another feels, to read both verbal and non-verbal body language. All of the units in this guide will provide activities to develop this "emotional attunement."

5. **PEOPLE SKILLS** It is the ability to get along with others—not your IQ—that determines success in life. People skills allow students to communicate and work cooperatively in group situations. The units on listening, giving put-ups (compliments), sharing and manners will help students fine-tune these social skills.

OVERVIEW OF SOCIAL SKILL UNITS

The units that follow are designed to assist in the development of social skills through:

direct instruction
practice and reinforcement
transfer of training

The units are designed to be used with *The Get-Alongs*, a series of social skill trade books for children in the primary grades. The unit components and activities, however, are applicable to the upper grades as well.

Each unit should take approximately one month to teach.   Plan between 30 and 45 minutes for the first day and between 5 and 10 minutes for the following days. The components are listed below, then defined in the next section. Words a teacher might use for the lesson are printed in *italics*.

The first day of the unit:

1. Introduce the social skill to class
2. Literature selection (i.e. social skill book, poem)
3. Fill in T-chart

Each unit will provide practice activities and sponges for the remainder of the month. Pick one activity or sponge per day.

4. **Sponges**
5. **Practice activities**

Also included are reinforcement activities to be used throughout the month:

6. **Quotations, poems, audio tapes**
7. **Goal cards (to celebrate success)**
8. **Transfer of training**
9. **Integrating the social skill with existing curriculum**

LESSON COMPONENTS

INTRODUCE THE SOCIAL SKILL TO CLASS

The purpose of this component is to hook the learner's past experiences to the social skill being taught. By actively involving the learners at the beginning of the lesson, naming the social skill objective, and explaining why it is important for all students, you make sure the class is mentally ready to begin the lesson. For example, if the social skill objective is listening, introductory questions might be:

Raise your hand if a teacher or family member has ever said to you, 'Won't you ever listen?'

Why did they say that? Why might it be important to listen? Think of one time you were glad you listened. Tell your study buddy about this time.

In addition to this guide, the first page of each social skill book provides introductory questions for that particular lesson.

SOCIAL SKILL BOOK OR OTHER LITERATURE SELECTION

1. If you are using the social skill books with your class, now is the appropriate time to read the book for this unit. (The Get-Along series was prepared for primary-age children.) Prepare the class by having them predict what the book will be about by reading the title and looking at the cover.

The stories are predictable, and they are written in rhyme. Once your listeners have recognized these elements, let them fill in the last word in some of the rhymes. For example,

Won't you ever listen?
Listen to me.
Face to face, eye to eye,
Knee to ....

Each book has a predictable story structure: problem, events, solution, characters, and setting. Once the problem in the book has been identified, stop reading and let students predict the solution with their study buddies. At the conclusion of the story, let them compare their predictions with the story. Each book suggests an activity to help students practice identifying the elements of the story.

    2. For each social skill unit, additional literature selections are suggested—including suggestions for older students. When you are integrating literature with social skill teaching, remember that a balanced reading lesson includes:

- activation of background information (hook into learners' past experiences)
- strategy instruction (self-questioning, prediction, story grammar, etc.)
- shared reading experiences (partner reading, literature circles, etc.)

T-CHART

Looks like	Sounds like

A T-chart is a visual aid that lists what the social skill looks like and sounds like. It is called "T" because it visually resembles a "T"! To the left of the vertical line, list what the skill looks like; to the right, what it sounds like. Under the column "sounds like," you can write both the actual words of the skill ("I don't understand") and general descriptors (a calm voice). The social skill anger management uses a modified T-chart: what it feels like, looks like, and sounds like.

    In addition to filling in the T-chart, you might list the actual steps for using the social skill. This is helpful for both anger management and problem solving. The T-chart and/or list of steps should be displayed on a large poster during the month the class is studying the skill.

SPONGES

Sponges are short, filler activities that require very little preparation time. They take no more than five minutes of classroom time. Use them whenever there is potential dead time. Use them:

- at the end of the morning or day
- during any transition (change of activity)
- when students are waiting (for anything!)

You may use the sponges listed in each unit as
- journal entries (e.g., for learning logs)
- notes written on a piece of paper that is handed to the teacher as a "ticket out the door"
- short discussion topics (begin sponge, throw koosh ball to a student to finish it)
- cooperative learning topics (provide the sponge and have students discuss in their groups)

PRACTICE ACTIVITIES

Following the list of sponges for each unit are many practice activities. Don't expect to use all of the activities. Rather, pick those most appropriate for your class. The activities will take anywhere from five to ten minutes. Our goal is that you provide at least one sponge or practice activity each day for about one month.

CLASS MEETINGS

Have a regularly scheduled meeting, with students sitting in a tight circle, to discuss social skill issues. The ground rules are that no names are to be used and no blaming or fault finding is allowed. The goal of the meeting is to collectively solve a social problem students may be having on the playground, outside or inside of school. Often a koosh ball or Native American talking stick is passed from student to student in the circle to indicate who the speaker is. A student may either make a contribution or pass. The teacher's function is to facilitate the process, not pass judgment. The topic for the discussion may be student or teacher determined and is often posted on the board in advance.

QUOTATIONS

Quotations are provided at the end of each unit that can be used in a variety of ways to remind students of the social skill of the month:
- Design charts or posters to hang in the classroom and hall.
- Use as prompts for journal writing.
- Develop hand or body motions to match the words.
- Design a march or dance to perform with it.
- Include quotes in a monthly newsletter to parents.

- Use them as cheers, similar to the cheers heard at a high school football game. Select a cheerleader to lead the class.

(Many of the original sources of the quotations are unknown to me, as I have been collecting them for many years. Whenever possible, however, I have cited the source.)

POEMS

At the end of each social skill book (in the *Get-Alongs*) is a poem that can be used in many of the ways you would use the quotations described above. Permission is granted to make copies of the last page of each social skill book to distribute to students. When children have memorized the poem, let them color the picture and take it home. Below are specific examples of how to use the poem in class:

• *Won't You Ever Listen?:* This poem lends itself to role playing. Children can point to face, eyes, and knees (in verse #1), nod their heads (verse #3), or raise their hands (verse #4).

• *Sticks & Stones:* The first verse ("Give a put-up and not a put-down/Wear a smile and not a frown") can be sung as a round using the music from the audio tape (available with each book).

• *A Win-Win Day:* Use the thumbs up and thumbs down hand motions for the verse, "I'll make it win-win, not lose-lose" lines of the poem.

• *I'm Always in Trouble:* Both hand and body movements work well with this poem. Students may actually role play the message.

AUDIO TAPES

The audio tapes for these books have both a spoken version as well as the text set to music. These audio tapes can be used in a variety of ways.

- At a listening center: Students can listen to the story again.
- Integrated with music instruction: Children can use musical instruments to accompany the songs, learn to sing along, or devise their own production.
- Children experiencing behavioral problems related to a specific social skill can go to the "Solution Corner." They listen to the story again, then write out their own action plan. Using the problem solving template (in reproducible

section), students can practice transferring the use of the social skill to their own particular problems.

GOAL CARDS

To help students be conscious of using the social skill, have them mark a goal card each time they use the skill. Goal cards are found in the last section of this guide book. Copy goal cards onto brightly colored, light-weight tag. Four cards can be made from one 8 1/2" x 11" sheet of paper.

- Select a goal card that is appropriate for the social skill you are teaching. Students can record the number of put-ups (compliments) given, times they shared, how many times they controlled their anger, or solved a problem.
- Consider the number of "points" available on the goal card. Early in the year or at the beginning of a new social skill lesson, use a card with fewer points so that it can be filled in less time. For a skill like giving put-ups that can be used many times during the day, use a card with more point opportunities. For a skill like anger management that is likely to be used less often, use a card with fewer response opportunities.
- Tape the goal card to the corner of each child's desk. Some teachers prefer to keep goal cards in a folder in the desk or taped to the inside of the desk lid.
- Explain to the class that they will give themselves a point (color in a segment) each time they use a skill. When students are just beginning to use a goal card, the teacher should initiate the awarding of points. For example, in the middle of a lesson, the teacher might say: *You were all such good listeners, sitting eye to eye and face to face, award yourselves a listening point.* Or, at the end of the day: *If you gave someone a put-up today, whisper what it was to your study buddy. Give yourself a point on your goal card.*

As students become accustomed to goal cards, let them award themselves points. It is always helpful, and raises accountability, to have students explain to their partners why they are giving themselves a point.

Should you reward students for filling out a goal card? Ideally, the act of keeping track of using the social skill should be intrinsically rewarding. When goal cards are completed, encourage students to take them home to show their families. Or let students accumulate 8 to10 cards and bind them together into a book titled *"I'm a Winner."*

If your class has been *hooked* on extrinsic rewards, you may have to offer a special privilege as recognition of card completion. For example, as students complete a certain number of cards (perhaps 8 cards), they may each pick a special privilege from a menu of privileges. Have the list of privileges on a chart or card. It might look like the menu below. Avoid rewards that must be purchased! Please note, however, that this author believes that having to bribe students to demonstrate prosocial behavior undermines their intrinsic motivation to use that behavior in other situations. Remember the old quote, "When we are truly giving to others, we do so without expecting a reward in return."

MENU OF PRIVILEGES

phone home	receive "happygram"
sit by friend for a day	be table captain
choose an art project	clean tables
pass out papers	bring favorite toy to school
inspect toys	feed pets
clean boards	have 5 minutes of free-time
read a story to class	sit in teacher's chair for a day
lead pledge	eat lunch in room with teacher
file papers	listen to music of choice
be last in line	be first in line
clean erasers	have computer time
visit principal	student suggestion:

TRANSFER OF TRAINING
As students internalize the social skill, provide opportunities for them to use the skill in natural settings.

HOMEWORK COUPONS
Homework coupons can be sent home each week. Introduce the coupons to parents with a letter describing their purpose. A model of such a letter is provided in the reproducible section of this guide book.

Encourage students to return the coupon within the same week. Perhaps the returned coupon could be used as a ticket to share during a class meeting or social skill discussion.

CROSS-AGE TUTORING

When President Kennedy said, "Ask not what your country can do for you; ask what you can do for your country," he was reminding us that helping others is the glue that bonds us together as a country. Giving students the opportunity to volunteer to help other kids learn not only lets them demonstrate a willingness to share (a social skill) but also gives them the opportunity to practice other prosocial behaviors (i.e. listening, giving put-ups, problem solving). Set up a "Future Teachers of America" program in your building where upper grade students can volunteer to help primary age students the last half hour of the school day. Develop an application process where students list their academic strengths and languages spoken. Prepare a contract for volunteers to sign that includes:
- a promise to follow through with their responsibility
- an agreement to keep information confidential
- an understanding of the importance of being on time and reliable
- an agreement to keep up with their own assignments

Provide monthly inservice for the cross-age volunteers to review both tutoring techniques and social skills.

INTEGRATING SOCIAL SKILLS

When developing a thematic, integrated unit it is natural to connect the theme across the disciplines (i.e. math, reading, writing, science, social studies, art, music). Now, add to the list of connections: social skill connections. For example, if your class is studying westward expansion in the U.S., identify the social skills that contributed to successful expansion. One middle school unit on "Perspectives" included a strand on empathy or recognizing feelings. A primary unit, Community, included the guiding questions
- What defines a community?
- How can a community meet the needs of its members?
- What are some problems communities face?
- How do people in communities work together to solve problems?

The development of each guiding question included social skill teaching. Problem solving and sharing were the focal points.

Another thematic unit, Relationships, included the familiar science connections (i.e. seasons, magnets, plants and animals), math connections (i.e. number families, measurement, telling time), and social studies connections (i.e., families, friends). The social skill highlighted for this unit was manners. Students studied

- telling time to be on time (vs. being late and rude)
- measuring to divide into equal parts and sharing
- ordinal number (1st, 2nd) and manners
- manners and cultural differences
- making friends, losing friends, and manners

In addition, the manners unit on the next page was used.

PLANNING A SOCIAL SKILL UNIT

A month-long planning sheet is included at the end of each unit. This guide is useful whether you are selecting a social skill to integrate with your thematic unit or simply as a "skill of the month." Many schools identify a "skill of the month" for emphasis *schoolwide*. For example, a social skill calendar may be developed by the faculty:

September	Listening
October	Problem Solving
November	Tattling vs. Reporting
December	Sharing
January	Anger Management
February	Put-ups (compliments)
March	Feelings
April	Manners

The teachers, specialists, principal, and assistants are all teaching the same skill. Bulletin boards, school newsletters, and assemblies support this skill. An even more powerful approach is when there is a school-community bond in developing a social skill agenda. (For more examples and information contact the Character Education Partnership, 809 Franklin Street, Alexandria, VA 22314.)

The following is an example of a monthly plan to teach manners. Blank guides are provided for each unit in this guide.

Social Skill: Manners

Month: January

Monday	Tuesday	Wednesday	Thursday	Friday
Introduction/Set: Word Sort; name columns Literature: *Copy the Cat* T-chart: w/class; label *Rude Dude/Polite Knight*	Motto//Quote/Song: "MANNERS ARE MARVELOUS"; learn Manners Rap	Class Meeting Topic: How can we use manners on the playground? (pass Koosh ball around circle)	Sponge: Journal—You would be my best friend if....	Class Meeting Topic: How can we use manners at an assembly?
Practice: Create a "Marvelous Manners" flip book, one page for each day of week; record examples of manners you use each day.	Sponge: Journal—List ways you could show manners to a guest teacher.	Class Meeting Topic: Introduce the person sitting next to you in the circle.	Sponge: Journal—When someone is rude to me I feel....	Class Meeting Topic: If a student is being rude while someone else is talking, what should we do? Share flip books "Marvelous Manners"
Practice: Graffiti Carousel—make graffiti charts for rude dudes in class, on playground, on bus, at lunch, in line	Sponge: Journal— Brainstorm a list of polite words.	Class Meeting Topic: What does this mean to you: "Kindness given is never lost."	Sponge: Journal—People are rude when they....	Class Meeting Topic: Name a time when someone was rude to you. NO NAMES!
Practice: Art project— make a posted "Wanted—a friend who...."	Sponge: Read *Random Acts of Kindness*; Journal—I practiced a random act of kindness when I...	Class Meeting Topic: Thank a class member for a random act of kindness.	Sponge: Read *Please* by Alicia Aspinwall; have students tally the number of times they hear 'please' during the day	Celebration/Closure: -Plan a class party invite guests brainstorm all the opportunities for using manners

CLASS MEETING: A CHANCE TO PRACTICE PROBLEM SOLVING TOGETHER.

SOLUTION TABLE: AN OPPORTUNITY FOR TRANSFER OF TRAINING. TWO STUDENTS CAN PROBLEM SOLVE.

LISTENING

Social skill book: *Won't You Ever Listen?*

DIRECTIONS

Plan approximately one month for the unit. On Day 1, introduce the skill, read related social skill book or poem, and make a T-chart with the class. For the remainder of the month, take 5 to 10 minutes a day for at least one practice or sponge activity.

INTRODUCE THE SOCIAL SKILL TO CLASS

Has anyone ever said to you, 'Won't you ever listen?' Who said it? Why did they want you to listen? What might have happened if you didn't listen?

SOCIAL SKILL BOOK

Let's predict what this story is going to be about. Who are the characters? What do you think is happening in the picture? Read the book. Ask the story comprehension questions from page 1 as you read.

ADDITIONAL LITERATURE SELECTIONS

Bennett, W. *The Book of Virtues*
        p. 44: Our Lips and Ears
        p. 32-33: To the Little Girl Who Wriggles
Cameron, A. *The Stories Julian Tells*
Cosgrove, S. *Gabby*
Geras, A. *My Grandmother's Stories: A Collection of Jewish Folktales*
Silverstein, S. *Falling Up*
        p. 38: The Voice
        p. 161: Headphone Harold
Silverstein, S. *A Light in the Attic*
        p. 95: The Little Boy and the Old Man

T-CHART

Stomper learned how to listen. Let's write down what he learned. What does listening look like and sound like? Fill out the T-chart as students give you examples.

Listening

Looks like	Sounds like
Eye to eye	Quiet
Knee to knee	Not talking while speaker is
Face to face	Asking a question if you need to
Nodding your head	"Yes" "OK"

Prepare a T-chart for not listening, too.

Not listening

Looks like	Sounds like
Not looking at speaker	Interrupting
Turning body away from speaker	Putting speaker down
Playing with things	Monopolizing conversation
Fidgeting	"That's dumb"

SPONGES

List the times when listening is important.
List the times when listening is important in school.
List the times when listening is important at home.
When did you listen today?
What might happen if you don't listen?
Describe a time you are glad you listened.
Describe a time when you wish you'd listened better.
Who listens to you?
List the people you've listened to today.
Brainstorm all the times you will need to listen in one day.
When might it be dangerous not to listen?
When someone doesn't listen to me, I feel....
I can tell someone isn't listening to me when they....

I can tell someone is listening to me when they....
If I didn't listen to my teacher, my teacher would feel....

PRACTICE ACTIVITIES

Look at me: Memorize (or read from note cards) a poem that you can say to your class. Or, use the following poem ("Apples of Gold" by J. Petty).

> Laugh a little - sing a little
> As you go your way!
> Work a little - play a little
> Do this every day!
>
> Give a little - take a little,
> Never mind a frown -
> Make your smile a welcomed thing
> All around the town!
>
> Laugh a little - love a little,
> Skies are always blue!
> Every cloud has silver linings,
> But it's up to you!

Recite the poem first with your back to the class; then recite it facing the class. Ask: *Which time was it easier for you to listen? Why?* Recite the poem again, first with your eyes looking down (not at the class), then with good eye contact (scanning entire class). *What was the difference this time? When were you doing your best listening? Why?*

Have partners practice talking to one another for one minute each, sitting back to back.

Partner #1

1. Lists favorite foods
2. Listens

Partner #2

1. Listens
2. Lists favorite games at school

Discuss: *How did you feel while talking and sitting back to back? How did you feel when you were listening but couldn't see the speaker's face?* Repeat this exercise having partners face each other, giving them different topics (e.g., favorite TV program). *Why is it better talking face to face and eye to eye?*

Inside circle/outside circle: Divide the class in half. Form two circles, one inside the other. Circles rotate in opposite directions while music is playing. When the music stops, students stop walking, turn, and each shakes the hand of the person facing him in the other circle. The teacher names a topic, and these new partners discuss it. When being the listener, a partner practices head nodding. Possible topics: favorite TV show, school subject, move, ice cream, animal, book.

The mike: Collect enough cardboard tubes from empty rolls of paper towels or toilet paper for half the class. Paint or cover tubes with construction paper to look like microphones. Explain that only the person with the microphone in hand can talk during the small group discussion. If someone else wants to talk, she must raise her hand and the speaker will pass the microphone. Discussion groups of no more than 4 students are given topics or questions. Begin with short discussion times and easy topics then progress to longer, more complicated discussions.

- *What do you like to play during recess? at home? on the weekend?*
- *What is your favorite school lunch? least favorite?*
- When reading a story to the class, stop periodically to ask comprehension questions, using this mike activity. *Who is your favorite character? What do you think will happen next?*

Gossip: Explain that sometimes when students are listening, they can't remember everything that is said. Demonstrate this by putting the following story on a tape recorder:

"Stomper had nine friends at his birthday party. They all brought presents they knew Stomper would like: bananas, balloons, apples, and bubble bath. After opening the presents they played games like musical chairs, tag, and Gossip. Stretch won two of the games. His prizes were a candy bar and an orange. The party was over at 4:00."

Only one student in the class gets to listen to the story, using headphones so no one else hears. That student whispers what he remembers of the story to the next person in a circle of 5 or 6 students. Ask the last person hearing the story to repeat it back into the tape recorder. Play the original version and new version. Discuss the differences. This game is even more fun if you have enough tape recorders for several groups to pass the story around at the same time. Notice how many different versions of the story are retold.

Discuss: *What can a good listener do to try to remember more of what he is listening to? Why might questioning the speaker help?*

What would you ask? This exercise is to help students learn how to ask questions when listening. *Have you ever been listening to someone talk and needed to ask them a question? We're going to practice asking questions. To show that we were listening, our question must be about what the speaker was saying. Good listeners ask good questions.* Write the statements listed below on the chalkboard. Then give the class two possible questions. Ask them to tell you which is the best match.

1. I can't find my favorite toy.
    a. Do you like chocolate cake? or,
    b. What toy are you looking for?
2. You'll miss the field trip if you don't bring everything back.
    a. What am I supposed to bring back? or,
    b. What's for lunch?
3. Wow! Today has been a great day!
    a. What made it a great day for you? or,
    b. Do you have any pets?

Next, the teacher talks a minute, then tells the class to ask a question. When the class understands how to ask good questions, partners can take turns asking the questions.

Simon says: Tell students to perform an activity. They must do it if your directions include the words "*Simon says;*" they should not follow the directions if they don't hear those words. Students who follow the directions when the teacher doesn't say *"Simon says"* must sit down. At the end of the game, applaud those left standing.

Guess what? *You're going to be sound detectives. The only sense you can use is your ears. Put your heads down on your desk, close your eyes, and listen. When you can identify the sound, raise your hand.* Use sounds available in your room:

clap your hands	close cupboard door	turn on a faucet
drop a pencil	sharpen a pencil	drum fingers on table
open/close a book	close a desk drawer	use a stapler
cut paper w/scissors	pour water into glass	knock on the door
hum	whistle	snap fingers

21

Punctuate my sentence! Explain that a good listener hears more than just words. A good listener can tell from the sound of the voice if a speaker is asking a question, making a telling statement, or issuing a command. Teach students how to form each punctuation mark (?, ., !) with a hand against their chests.

      Period: closed fist
      Exclamation point: hold pointer finger up
      Question mark: form a c with thumb and pointer finger

Model tone of voice for a statement with a soft, normal voice; a question with a questioning sound; a command with a loud, firm voice (perhaps even angry). Use these words, with 3 different intonations:

Be nice.	Be nice!	Be nice?
Give it to me.	Give it to me!	Give it to me?
Not me.	Not me!	Not me?

When class understands the distinctions, let them work with partners. Write the following words on the chalkboard: No, Say thank you, You did, Please, OK. Partners take turns testing each other.

Listening poster: Draw the outline of a large hand on a poster for your room. On the thumb and each finger, draw a pictograph of the steps in good listening. For example: (1) eye, (2) ear, (3) closed mouth, (4) 2 chairs facing each other, (5) hand up (to ask a question).

QUOTATIONS

The secret of being a bore is to tell everything. (Voltaire)

Bore: a person who talks when you wish him to listen.

Before you can listen to learn,
You must learn to listen.

Lend me your ears!

Listening is hard work.

For most people the opposite of talking isn't listening, it's waiting.

LISTENING

If my eyes you cannot see, don't begin to talk to me.

You have two ears and one mouth. You need to listen twice as much as you speak.

Honor people with your attention, not your opinions.

We are more likely to impress people if we employ our ears, not our mouth. (Kin Hubbard)

GOAL CARDS

Have several goal cards ready for students to record each time they listen. Examples of goal cards in the reproducible section to measure listening skills: "Pay yourself 1¢" and "Tune in to listening."

HOMEWORK COUPONS

Send home a coupon every few days during the month to transfer the skill of listening.

"GIVE ME FIVE"
WHAT A GOOD LISTENER LOOKS AND SOUNDS LIKE.

Monday	Tuesday	Wednesday	Thursday	Friday
Introduction Set: Literature: T-chart:	Motto/Quote/ Song:	Class Meeting:	Sponge:	Class Meeting:
Practice:	Sponge:	Class Meeting:	Sponge:	Class Meeting:
Practice:	Sponge:	Class Meeting:	Sponge:	Class Meeting:
Practice:	Sponge:	Class Meeting:	Sponge:	Class Meeting:

GiViNG PUT-UPS
(COMPLiMENTS)
Social skill book: *Sticks & Stones*

DiRECTiONS
Plan approximately one month for the unit. On Day 1, introduce the skill, read the social skill book, and fill in a T-chart with the class. For the remainder of the month, take 5 to10 minutes a day to complete at least one sponge or practice activity.

iNTRODUCE THE SOCiAL SKiLL TO CLASS
What words can people say to you that make you feel good? What do people say to you that hurts your feelings? If we call words that hurt your feelings a put-down, what might we call words that make you feel good? Yes, a put-up is another word for a compliment. Which person would you rather have as a friend, the one giving the put-up or the person giving the put-down?

SOCiAL SKiLL BOOK
Let's predict what this book will be about from the title. How many of you know the verse "Sticks and Stones"? Let's say the verse together: Sticks and stones may break my bones but words will never hurt me. Do you think this is true? Nod your head yes or shake it no. Read the book. Ask the story comprehension questions included on the first page.

ADDiTiONAL LiTERATURE SELECTiONS

Bennett, W. *The Book of Virtues*
    p. 110: Little Sunshine
    p. 112: Diamonds and Toads
    p. 118: Androcles and the Lion
    p. 207: If You Were
    p. 341: The Arrow and the Song
Blume, J. *Blubber*
Conly, J. *Crazy Lady*
Cosgrove, S. *Sassafras*
Lowry, L. *Number the Stars*

Mazer, N. *Mrs. Fish, Ape & Me, the Dump Queen*

T-CHART

Let's fill in a T-chart of put-ups, the way Ribit learned to give them. Remember, you can give put-up without using words, too.

Put-up (compliment)

Looks like	Sounds like
smile	"That's great."
nod	"You're fast in math."
thumbs up	"Yeah!"
pat on the back	"Awesome."
applauding	"You have a nice smile."
'OK' sign with finger/thumb	"That was nice of you to help."

You may also choose to prepare a T-chart on put-downs for contrast.

Put-down

Looks like	Sounds like
frown	"Yuk."
wrinkled nose	"That's dumb."
thumbs down	"Your work looks awful."

SPONGES

When someone smiles at me, I....
Put-ups I'd like to hear from adults are....
Put-ups I'd like to hear from my friends are....
The people I could give a put-up to today are....
When I get a put-up, I feel....
When I get a put-down, I feel....
These are the words that make me feel good:
Here's a list of all the nice things I've done today:
My teacher gives me a put-up when....
One put-up I received today was....

GIVING PUT-UPS

To encourage intrinsic motivation, have students give themselves put-ups:
One time when I was nice at school I....
One random act of kindness I did was....
Something I do that I am proud of is....
I make other people happy when I....
These are all the things I do well at school:
These are the people who think I am special:

PRACTICE ACTIVITIES

Plus & minus: In small groups (or whole class for early primary), make a chart describing the pluses of giving put-ups and the minuses of giving put-downs.

+ Giving put-ups +	- Giving put-downs -
makes friends	breaks friendships
makes a person feel good	hurts feelings
shows respect	shows lack of respect

Kindness is a chain reaction: Cut colored strips of paper to make a paper chain. For example, a strip 1.5" x 11" is a good size. When students want to compliment one another, they write the put-up on a strip, fold and paste it to the growing chain hanging in your classroom.

If you meet a person without a smile, give him one of yours: Have students conduct an experiment, smiling at someone at school they do not know. Ask them to report back what happened after they smiled.

You can have this, but you can't have that: Play this categories game with a koosh ball. Initiate the game by giving at least two examples, then throw the ball to a student who wants to add another example (without naming the categories). Name the categories you can and can't have only when the game is over. Here is how you might begin the game when the categories are put-ups and put-downs:

You can have a thumbs up, but you can't have a thumbs down.
You can have "nice job," but you can't have "that's ugly."
You can have a wink, but you can't have a frown.

Put-up tree: On a wall or bulletin board, hang a paper tree without leaves. Add leaves or decorate the tree with put-ups as the seasons and/or holidays change. For example, on Monday you might have students draw names out of a hat for a secret pal. During the week they secretly watch their pal to decide on a put-up to give him. On Friday, the art project is to construct the tree decoration on which their put-ups are written. Put-ups remain on the tree until the tree is redecorated the following month. Examples for a monthly theme might be:

- September tree has fall leaves. ("A positive pile of put-ups.")
- October tree has a pumpkin patch below it. ("Put-up patch.")
- November tree has thank you notes attached. ("Thanking tree.")
- December tree has mock packages under it with put-ups written to students. ("Gifts of words.")

Adapt a song—"Three Blind Mice": Sing the following verse to the tune of "Three Blind Mice":

> *Three kind kids.   Three kind kids.*
> *See how they smile.   See how they smile.*
> *They give put-ups and not put downs.*
> *They wear a smile and not a frown.*
> *They make new friends all around the town. They're*
> *Three kind kids.*

Adjective hunt: Supply a list of adjectives. Let each student pick three adjectives that best describe his partner (or team members). To encourage specific put-ups, you can supply the format:
_____ is _____ because_____.
For example, "Jason is polite because he always says thank you."

agreeable	brave	bubbly	caring
cooperative	clever	dependable	energetic
enjoyable	enthusiastic	expert	fair
friendly	fun	fantastic	great
good	gentle	handy	happy
helpful	honest	interesting	musical
outgoing	observant	original	pleasant
pretty	positive	quiet	respectful
smiling	special	strong	thoughtful
truthful	terrific	trustworthy	understanding
unselfish	valuable	wise	wonderful

28

Name tag messages: If students have laminated name tags on their desks, write a surprise personalized put-up to each child with a washable marker. Write a new put-up each Monday morning during the month you are working on this skill. Collect specific examples of student behavior during the week on a clipboard as you monitor your class. For example: Tanya was thoughtful when she shared her crayons with Rick. Students can wash off the put-up on Friday, in preparation for Monday's new compliment.

Word cache: A cache is a place for storing treasures. In this case, the treasures are put-ups. With the class, create a chart that describes the three types of put-ups one can give. Continue to add to this cache all week. This will assist students in developing variety and specificity in giving put-ups.

Actions	Work	Looks/dresses
helpful	neat	neat, curly hair
polite	careful printing	pretty smile
thoughtful	fast with math facts	cheerful
good sport	writes exciting stories	colorful shirt

QUOTATIONS

The right word spoken at the right time sometimes achieves miracles.

Speak kindly today; when tomorrow comes you will be in practice.

It is not fair to ask of others what you are not willing to do yourself. (Eleanor Roosevelt)

The music that can deepest reach
And cure all ill, is cordial speech. (Emerson)

No one cares how much you know
Until they know how much you care.

...no man can sincerely try to help another without helping himself. (Emerson)

It's hard to spread sunshine without getting some on yourself.

Be what you wish others to become.
Make yourself, not your words, a sermon. (Henri Frederic Amiel)

Be cheerful. Of all the things you wear, your expression is the most important.

What sunshine is to flowers, smiles are to humanity.

The best vitamin for making friends: B-1.

Smile...it takes only 13 muscles. A frown takes 64.

A smile is a loan that is always returned.

What you do not want done to yourself, do not do to others.
(Confucius)

If I can stop one heart from breaking, I shall not live in vain;
If I can ease one life the aching, Or cool one pain,
Or help one fainting robin unto his nest again,
I shall not live in vain. (Emily Dickinson)

GOAL CARDS

Let students give themselves a point (or color in a segment) every time they give a put-up to someone. Hold them accountable for accurate scoring by having them tell their study buddies what the put-up was. There are many goal cards for put-ups in the reproducible section: "Put-up scoreboard," "Light up our lives with put-ups," "Pay yourself 1¢," and "Give a ray of sunshine."

HOMEWORK COUPONS

Send home one coupon every few days during the month you are studying this social skill.

GIVING PUT-UPS

SOCIAL SKILL: GIVING COMPLIMENTS (PUT-UPS) MONTH:

Monday	Tuesday	Wednesday	Thursday	Friday
Introduction Set: Literature: T-chart:	Motto/Quote/Song:	Class Meeting:	Sponge:	Class Meeting:
Practice:	Sponge:	Class Meeting:	Sponge:	Class Meeting:
Practice:	Sponge:	Class Meeting:	Sponge:	Class Meeting:
Practice:	Sponge:	Class Meeting:	Sponge:	Class Meeting:

GIVING PUT-UPS

PUT-UPS
HOW MANY WAYS CAN WE GIVE PUT-UPS?

THIS MAKES ME SMILE

SUE JILL BOBBY EMIL JA

MIA SAM JOEY RASHID GI

GIVING PUT-UPS

PROBLEM SOLVING

Social skill book: *A Win-Win Day*

DIRECTIONS

Plan approximately one month for the unit. On Day 1, introduce the skill, read the social skill book, and present the steps in problem solving.

1. Describe the problem.
2. Brainstorm several choices you have for solving it.
3. Describe the consequences of making each choice.
4. Select the best choice.

For the remainder of the month, take 5 to 10 minutes each day for at least one practice or sponge activity.

INTRODUCE THE SOCIAL SKILL TO CLASS

Have you ever had a problem? What was it? Write "problem" on the board. Define problem as something you don't know the answer to right away. Compare to problems in math. *In math you are given problems like 10 + 5 = ? Your job is to find the answer. You also have problems in your life when you try to find the right answer. You may have problems on the playground, problems with doing your work, or problems with your toys. If you have a broken toy, you try to figure out how to fix it. If your ball is taken by someone else on the playground, you want to figure out the best way to get it back. We're going to call this "problem solving." You want to find a good solution to your problem, not one that will cause another problem.*

SOCIAL SKILL BOOK

Let's look at the title of this book. What do you think a "win-win day" is? What would a "lose-lose" day be? In this book, Billy learns how to become a good problem solver so he can have a "win-win day." Read the book; ask the story comprehension questions included on the first page.

ADDITIONAL LITERATURE SELECTIONS

Bennett, W. *The Book of Virtues*
> *p. 357: The Three Little Pigs*
> *p. 370: The Farmer and His Sons*
> *p. 418: Kill Devil Hill*

p. 446: How the Little Kite Learned to Fly
p. 533: The Little Hero of Holland
p. 536: You Mustn't Quit
p. 567: Can't
Blume, J. *Superfudge*
Browne, A. *The Piggybook*
Bunting, E. *The Wednesday Surprise*
Carlson, N. *Arnie and the Stolen Markers*
Cosgrove, S. *Little Mouse on the Prairie*
Giff, P. *The Girl Who Knew It All*
McPhail, D. *Lost!*
Pfeffer, S. *What Do You Do When Your Mouth Won't Open?*
Phelan, T. *The Week Mom Unplugged the TV*
Skurzynski, G. *Martin By Himself*

T-CHART

Let's list the steps Billy followed when he wanted to solve a problem. First, he knew he had a problem. Then he thought of all the things he could try to solve his problem. Then he thought about what would happen with each solution. He picked what he wanted to have happen to him, the best solution.

Problem:

Choices (things to try)	**Consequences** **Why?** **Why not?**	
1.	1.	1.
2.	2.	2.
3.	3.	3.

The solution I will pick is:

To model the problem-solving process, use this chart to illustrate how Billy solved each of his problems.

1. Problem: His brother hid the truck.
2. Problem: At the bus stop, his friends were throwing rocks.
3. Problem: In the lunch line, someone punches him.
4. Problem: In class, someone calls him a name.

PROBLEM SOLVING

Encourage students to think of 3 or more choices (things to try) for each problem.

SPONGES

One time I made a poor choice was when....
      I knew it was a poor choice because....
One time I made a good choice was when....
      I knew it was a good choice because....
I feel like a winner when....
Some choices I made by myself today were....
I had a problem when....
One problem I had this week....
One problem I couldn't solve by myself was....
I am a good problem solver because I....
If a student pushes you in the lunch line, what choices do you have?
List 3 choices you would have if someone spilled paint on your new
      shirt on purpose.
List 3 choices you would have if your best friend said she likes
      someone else better than you.
List 3 choices you have to help you remember your homework.
List 3 choices you have when other kids tell you that you can't play
with them.

PRACTICE ACTIVITIES

Daily problem solving: Select one problem a day to have the class practice the steps in problem solving. Move from whole group practice, to partner practice, to individual practice. Give students the choice of picking their own problem or using a teacher-selected problem. When students are ready for individual practice, prepare problem-solving pads for each student. A template is provided in the reproducible section.

Recognizing a problem: Below are several activities that help students recognize and define a problem.

    Mystery bag: Have a bag (such as an old pillow case or shopping bag) filled with various items (e.g., a ball, a pencil, a sock, a coin). One child comes up and draws out an item. Working with partners, brainstorm all the possible problems that could be caused by that item. The child who drew the item calls on students for their examples of problems related to that item.

PROBLEM SOLVING

Magazine/newspaper problems: Let partners canvas magazines or newspapers for pictures that suggest someone has a problem. They cut out the picture and write or tell class what the problem might be. Make a collage of these real life problems.

Mapping problems: Let small groups do a mind map of problems. Get the groups started by categorizing places students may encounter problems: playground, hall, cafeteria, bus, after school, library, playing with a friend. Students continue by describing the types of problems they might encounter in these places.

Taking responsibility for the problem: If students can blame someone else for the problem, they don't have to solve it. Below are a series of activities to help students take ownership of the problem.

I statements: Explain to class that "I" statements help you recognize the problem. Blame statements won't help you solve problems. The words "you" and "it" are often in blame statements. Good problem solvers take responsibility for their actions. Read the following statements to class. Have them point to themselves for "I" statements (taking responsibility) and point to you if it's a "blame" statement.

- *You did it to me.*
- *It fell off the table.*
- *I bumped into it and it fell.*
- *My mom threw it away.*
- *I lost my homework.*
- *My brother made me do it.*

Let students brainstorm examples of "I" statements and blame statements. Then give the following list of blame statements to students working in partnerships. Let them take turns changing the list into "I" statements.

- *My homework is lost.*
- *It's not my fault that I'm late.*
- *Jason told me I didn't have to do it.*
- *Andy hit me first so I hit him back.*
- *She keeps bugging me so I can't get my work done.*

Identifying choices and consequences: The following activities help students brainstorm the choices they have when solving problems.

Inside circle/Outside circle: Divide the class in half. Each half forms a circle, one circle inside the other. The inside circle faces the outside circle, so that children are paired. Describe a problem (e.g., *You lost your lunch money.*). The outside circle partner gives one choice (thing to try). The inside circle partner identifies consequence of that choice. Then reverse roles: Inside circle partner gives a choice (thing to try); outside circle partner identifies the consequence. Then rotate the circle (e.g., *outside circle rotate three people to your left*) and give a new problem (e.g., *When you got home from school the door was locked to your house. You don't have a key. What choices do you have?*).

Rural mail box: Set up a rural mail box (with a red flag along its side). Beside it place a stack of paper with the words: "Dear Abby, My problem is...." When students want help with solving a problem, they finish the letter and mail it to "Dear Abby." That is, they place the letter in the mail box and turn the red flag up. Names are optional. Once a week have a class meeting to discuss choices and consequences for each problem.

"And then": Describe a problem situation. Call on a student to suggest a solution. Use a koosh ball for this activity. Each student throws the koosh ball to another student who continues to describe the chain of events, beginning each statement with "And then..." For example: You lost your lunch money on the way to school.

> Student #1: "And then, I walked back home to get more."
> Student #2: "And then, I was late getting to school."
> Student #3: "And then, I had to go to the office."

"And then..." Flip Book: Form flip book by arranging 3 sheets of paper so that side edges are even but bottom edges are one inch apart. Fold top sheet so it is one inch from bottom; then fold second and third sheets so that you end up with a 6-page flip book. Children write "And then...." stories. Page one begins with the description of the problem (e.g., Jan knocked my book down.). Pages 2, 3, 4, 5, and 6 begin with the words "And then" to describe the sequence of consequences that solution might have (e.g., And then I knocked hers down, too. And then she hit me. And then I hit her back. And then the teacher was so angry she sent us to the office.). Students illustrate their stories.

Numbered heads: With cooperative groups of 3 or 4 students, students number off in each group (1,2,3...). Present a problem situation. Say, *Heads together. Use the problem-solving model. Pick the choice you think has the best consequence.* Give groups time to process the problem. Then say, *Heads up. Threes up.* (Or, Twos up, Ones up) All #3s stand. Call on students standing to present their group's choice and consequence. Situations to use:

PROBLEM SOLVING

- One person on your team refuses to cooperate. In fact, she won't even do her share of the work. You end up doing all of it. You don't think this is fair.
- On the way to school you see your friends teasing a little child who is your neighbor. The little child is crying.
- The boy who sits next to you in class is always taking your things. First he took your pencil; now, he has some of your crayons.
- You are in a cooperative team with three other students. They are all friends and always talking to each other. They don't pay any attention to you and even put down your ideas when you speak.

QUOTATIONS

The best way to escape from a problem is to solve it.
(Brendan Francis)

The man who gives up accomplishes nothing and is only a hindrance. The man who does not give up can move mountains. (Ernest Hello)

No one can predict to what heights you can soar. Even you will not know until you spread your wings.

You cannot discover new oceans unless you have the courage to lose sight of the shore.

One who lacks courage to start has already finished.

Failing to prepare, we prepare to fail.

Success comes in cans; failure comes in can'ts.

2/3 of promotion is motion.

People don't fail - they give up.

Some people dream of worthy accomplishments while others stay awake and do them.

The difference between dreams and reality is EFFORT.

Everyone makes mistakes. It is what you do afterwards that counts.

PROBLEM SOLVING

A first failure may pave the way for a later success.

Success is a dream turned into reality.

A man who has committed a mistake and doesn't correct it is committing another mistake. (Confucius)

Be not afraid of going slowly, be afraid only of standing still. (Chinese proverb)

If you blame others for your failures, do you credit others with your successes?

There isn't any map of the road to success; you have to find your own way.

ADDITIONAL LITERATURE SELECTIONS

Adolescent literature is a good source of stories about problem solving. Some favorites are:
Armstrong, W. *Sounder*
Speare, E. *Sign of the Beaver*
Stevenson, R. *Treasure Island*
Tayler, M. *Roll of Thunder, Hear My Cry*

GOAL CARDS

Use goal accomplishment cards to help students record when they try the problem-solving model. Younger students can color in a segment each time they use the model. Older students can list the problems with which they used the model. As students progress in their problem-solving ability, give them their own problem solving pads. The template is in the reproducible section. Examples of goal cards in the reproducible section for this social skill: "My goal is," "I think I can," "The difference between dreams and reality," and "Ideas won't work."

HOMEWORK COUPONS

Send home one coupon every few days to promote transfer of training.

PROBLEM SOLVING

Monday	Tuesday	Wednesday	Thursday	Friday
Introduction Set: Literature: T-chart:	Motto/Quote/ Song:	Class Meeting:	Sponge:	Class Meeting:
Practice:	Sponge:	Class Meeting:	Sponge:	Class Meeting:
Practice:	Sponge:	Class Meeting:	Sponge:	Class Meeting:
Practice:	Sponge:	Class Meeting:	Sponge:	Class Meeting:

ANGER MANAGEMENT

Social skill book: *I'm Always in Trouble*

DIRECTIONS

Plan approximately one month for the unit. On Day 1, introduce the skill, read the social skill book, and fill in a T-chart with the class. For the remainder of the month, take 5 to 10 minutes a day for at least one practice or sponge activity.

INTRODUCE SOCIAL SKILL TO CLASS

Have you ever seen someone who was angry? What did they look like? How does your body feel when you are angry? What do some people do when they are angry? Have you seen them hitting others or saying bad things? What's wrong with this? What could you do when you are angry but don't want to show it by hitting or saying bad things? Emphasize key concept: *Feeling angry is not bad, but acting angry may hurt people, create enemies, be dangerous, or destroy property. There are better ways to express your anger.*

SOCIAL SKILL BOOK

Let's predict what this book will be about from the title. Now, what clues do you see from the cover? Read the book. As you read, ask the story comprehension questions included on the first page.

ADDITIONAL LITERATURE SELECTIONS

Bennett, W. *The Book of Virtues*
      p. 37: The King and His Hawk
      p. 40: Anger
Bennett, W. *The Children's Book of Heroes*
      p. 29: Jackie Robinson
Brimner, L. *Cory Coleman.*
Crary, E. *When You're Mad and You Know It*
Mauser, P. *A Bundle of Sticks*
Riley, S. *Angry*
Silverstein, S. *Falling Up*
      p. 44: Screamin' Millie
Simon, N. *I Was So Mad!*
Wells, R. *Noisy Nora*

T-CHART

There were lots of things that made Derek mad or angry. What were they? How does your body talk to you to tell you that you are angry? Let's fill out a T-chart to show what anger looks like, sounds like, and feels like.

Anger

Feels like	Looks like	Sounds like
tense	clenched fists	saying bad things
fast heart beat	fighting	heavy breathing
hot or cold	throwing things	yelling, shouting
knots in stomach	frowning	"I hate you."
	red face	"You're dumb."

Discuss what some of the negative consequences are of showing your anger the way it's described in the T-chart. Use an if/then sequence:

    If someone yells or shouts, then....
    If someone says bad things, then....
    If someone throws things, then....

With the class, prepare a T-chart for calm (controlling anger).

Calm (controlling anger)

Feels like	Looks like	Sounds like
Relaxed	Peaceful, still	Calm voice
Breathing deeply	Maybe closed eyes	Counting to 10
Thinking nice things	Maybe head down	Self talk; "Calm down"
	Maybe walking away	"I can control it."

SPONGES

These are things that make me angry:
I controlled my anger when....
These are my anger warning signs:
When I'm angry I feel like.... But I don't because....
One time I wished I'd controlled my anger....

ANGER MANAGEMENT

The consequences of not controlling my anger at school are....
        at home are....
I like to control my anger by....
It doesn't pay to lose my temper because....
Make up your own simile. For example,
        Anger is like rough seas.
        Anger is like being sick.
        Anger is like a game.
        Anger is like the color red.
        He is as angry as a....

The best way to show my anger
        when someone takes my toy is....
        when someone bumps into me is....
        when someone calls me a name is....
        when someone crowds into the line is....
My friends would say I get angriest when....
I was maddest at school when....
I know my friend is angry when....
When I get angry
        on the playground, I can....
        at home, I can....
        in class, I can....
Draw a picture of what anger feels like and looks like.
I get angry at myself when....

PRACTICE ACTIVITIES

Calming down: Discuss with the class all of the options to consider when feeling angry. Perhaps the first step is to be calm before deciding which option to take. Some people get calm by

- taking deep breaths and counting to ten
- thinking of (picturing in their mind's eye) places that help them relax (e.g., the woods, the beach, a sunset)
- finding a quiet place to be, away from whatever triggered the anger
- saying nice things to themselves (see examples of quotations; let students pick their favorite one to repeat to themselves when trying to calm down)

Mad to calm: Ask students to role play body language that shows anger. While you count to ten, have them gradually change from looking mad to looking calm. Eventually have them role play being angry, counting to ten using self-talk, showing calm when they reach ten.

Adapt a song: Use the melody to the old song, "Are you sleeping? Are you sleeping? Brother John. Brother John." (Also known as Frére Jacques) Insert the following words:

Are you angry?	Are you angry?
Boys and girls.	Boys and girls.
Stop and count to ten.	Stop and count to ten.
Calm you'll be.	Calm you'll be.

Raggedy Ann & Andy: Practice tensing and relaxing one part of the body at a time. (e.g., *Tense your arms while I count to 3; now relax 1, 2, 3; tense your fists 1, 2, 3; roll your shoulders 1, 2, 3*) When you call *Raggedy Ann & Andy*, kids should drop to the ground like rag dolls.

Choosing to talk: Sometimes when we're angry, we decide to talk to the person who made us angry. Role play with one student how to use a calm voice when angry, talking in a way that won't make the other person angry too. List several situations on the board for partners to role play with each other. Afterwards, post a master list of verbal solutions to the problems.

Someone...
- grabs your ball away ("May I please have my ball back?")
- scribbles on your paper ("Please don't do that. I have an extra piece of paper if you'd like to draw on it.")
- won't give you a turn at four-square ("I'd like to take my turn now.")
- is being mean to your friend ("You really make me angry when you treat my friend that way.")
- is pestering you on the playground ("You are really bugging me. Please stop.")

Don't bug me: Each student draws a large bug outline. Within the bug, students write (or draw) what bugs them (makes them angry). Have them think of things that people do or say to them that make them angry.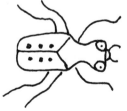

Collage: Using magazine pictures, create a collage of pictures showing anger (or situations that make you angry) and pictures showing calm (or places/situations that help you calm down).

Rap: Write a rap to chant in class for controlling anger.

Bubble cartoons: Students design their own cartoons showing a situation likely to produce angry feelings. Let them fill in the bubbles to show how they controlled the anger.

      Variation: give students pictures of situations that would make a student angry, then let them fill in the bubbles.

Channel your anger: Let cooperative groups design and act out a 3 minute television advertisement about anger management.

Corners: Select four examples or topics where anger management is critical. For example: SPORTS, WORLD EVENTS, TELEVISION (give name of one TV program students watch), or TRAFFIC. Label each corner of the room with a different topic. Students choose a corner. Each group prepares a chart describing:

    • Why people get angry in that situation.

    • What it looks like in this situation when you lose your temper.

    •Negative consequences of not controlling anger (for athletes, countries/leaders, actors, drivers) in this situation.

Variation: In early primary, chart one topic a day during whole group discussion. This can be repeated many times changing the topics: PLAYGROUND, AT HOME, TO/FROM SCHOOL, AT A FRIEND'S HOUSE.

You can have...(calm examples) but you can't have...(angry examples): This is fun to play with a koosh ball. Teacher begins the game by saying "You can have quiet but you can't have hitting. Who can give me the next example?" Throw the koosh ball to the next hand up. The ball continues to be passed around to students who can give examples. It might sound like:

    You can have counting to ten but you can't have pushing.

    You can have relaxing but you can't have biting.

    You can have deep breaths but you can't have name calling.

    You can have quiet but you can't have a tantrum.

QUOTATIONS

Frogs have it easy. They can eat what bugs them.

Some people develop eyestrain looking for trouble.

For of all sad words of tongue or pen,
The saddest are those: It might have been. (Whittier)

He who angers you conquers you! (Elizabeth Kenny)

The game of life is a game of boomerangs. Our thoughts, deeds, and words return to us sooner or later, with astounding accuracy. (Florence Scovel Shinn)

No person in the world ever attempted to wrong another without being injured in return, some way, somehow, sometime. (William George Jordan)

A minute of thought is worth more than an hour of talk.

The art of being wise is the art of knowing what to overlook.

Be sure your brain is in gear before engaging your mouth.

Words in haste do friendships waste.

Better to slip with the foot than with the tongue.

The longer you keep your temper the more it will improve.

GOAL CARDS

Have several goal cards ready for students to record each time they control their anger. Younger children can color in a segment each time. Older students can write "I controlled my anger when..." Examples of goal cards to measure this skill: "It is only through change that we grow," "Going in the right direction," and "Sailing along."

HOMEWORK COUPONS

As students work on anger management, send home one coupon every few days to promote transfer of training.

SOCIAL SKILL: ANGER MANAGEMENT   MONTH:

Monday	Tuesday	Wednesday	Thursday	Friday
Introduction Set: Literature: T-chart:	Motto/Quote/Song:	Class Meeting:	Sponge:	Class Meeting:
Practice:	Sponge:	Class Meeting:	Sponge:	Class Meeting:
Practice:	Sponge:	Class Meeting:	Sponge:	Class Meeting:
Practice:	Sponge:	Class Meeting:	Sponge:	Class Meeting:

When you're mad
About to fight,
Control your anger
With all your might!

Take deep breaths
Count to ten,
Before you try
To talk again.

If you can't use
A cool, calm voice,
To walk away
Is a better choice.

48   ANGER MANAGEMENT

SHARiNG
Social skill book: *Sharing is Caring*

DiRECTiONS
Plan approximately one month for the unit. On Day 1, introduce the skill, read the social skill book, and make a T-chart with the class. For the remainder of the month, take at least 5 to10 minutes a day to complete at least one sponge or practice activity.

INTRODUCE THE SOCIAL SKiLL TO CLASS
Has anyone every shared something with you? What did they share? How did you feel when they shared? Have you ever shared something? How did you feel? If students need prompts, ask: *Have you shared your toys with a friend? Have you offered a snack or some of your candy to a friend? Have you taken turns playing a game?*

SOCiAL SKiLL BOOK
First, let's predict what this book will be about from the title. What do the words "Sharing is Caring" mean to you? The picture on the cover will give you a clue. Read the book. Ask the story comprehension questions on the first page.

ADDiTiONAL LiTERATURE SELECTiONS
Bennett, W. *The Book of Virtues:*
    p. 122: The Legend of the Dipper
    p. 148: A Legend of the Northland
Bennett, W. *The Children's Book of Heroes:*
    p. 56: The Star Jewels
    p. 62: Mother Teresa
Goble, P. *The Gift of the Sacred Dog* (non-fiction)
Henkes, K. *Chester's Way*
Henwood, S. *A Piece of Luck*
Hoban, R. *A Birthday for Frances*
Larned, M. *Stone Soup for the World*
Mueller, V. *A Playhouse for a Monster*
Namioka, L. *Yang the Youngest and His Terrible Ear*
Silverstein, S. *The Giving Tree*
Silverstein, S. *Falling Up:*
    p. 50: Sharing

T-CHART

Let's make a T-chart to describe what it looks like and sounds like when we share.

Sharing

Looks like	Sounds like
Children taking turns	"Would you like to play?"
One person using a toy at a time	"It's your turn now."
2 kids using one box of crayons	"May I use the red next, please?"
Happy faces	"You can use this now."

SPONGES

When someone shares with me, I feel....
These are all the times I can take turns:
These are times when I don't have to take turns:
When someone doesn't share with me, I feel....
These are the times I can take turns on the playground:
At home, I can share....
These are things I shouldn't share:

PRACTICE ACTIVITIES

Vertical poetry: Write a vertical poem for sharing.

S
H
A
R
I
N
G

Koosh-ball: *If I throw the ball to you, name one thing you can share.*

Categories: Make a chart that categorizes the things that can be shared. Keep adding to the lists each day as children discover more things they can share. For example:

Time	Ideas	Turns	Skills
To listen Help pick up	With partner Class discussion	On slide With toys	Tutor Read to child

Spin the spinner: Make a cardboard game card with a spinner attached. Students take turns spinning. They must give an example of what they could share that fits the category the pointer stops on.

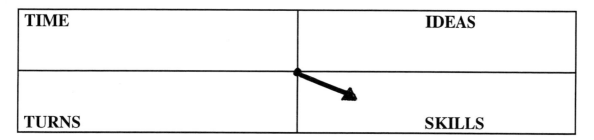

TIME	IDEAS
TURNS	SKILLS

Sharing things about "me":

1. Who am I? Arrange children into groups of four. Give each team member a 3 x 5 card to write 5 things about himself that makes him feel special. The team mixes the cards up. Each member draws a card and must guess who that card belongs to by writing their guess first, then telling the group.

2. How well do I know you? Working with a study buddy, each person fills out a card, telling what her favorites are and what she thinks her partner's favorites are. When cards are completed, partners compare answers to see how well they know each other.

	Me	My partner
favorite TV show		
favorite food		
favorite sport		
favorite ice cream		

3. Post a giant timeline on butcher paper or use the chalkboard. Students are invited to make an entry on the timeline any day that they wish. Choose a different theme each week. For example: good things that happened to me, surprises, funny things, firsts.

SHARING

Theme: *This is a first for me!*

May 10	May 11	May 12	May 13	May 14

Sharing in a cooperative TEAM:

T   Together
E   Everyone
A   Achieves
M   More

Below are ideas to practice the sharing of time and ideas when working in a cooperative team.

1. Chips can be used for small group discussions. Each child is given 3, 4, or 5 chips. Poker chips of different colors work well. When an individual member shares an idea with the group, he puts a chip in a cup in the center of the table. If he uses up all of his chips, he doesn't give another idea until all other team members have used their chips.

2. Teach class how to invite their teammates to share ideas. Write examples of invitations on the chalkboard as reminders.
   - What do you like about....
   - What do you want to do?
   - What do you think?

3. Have teams brainstorm solutions to sharing problems. Examples of topics might be:
   - How can you get other kids to share?
   - How can you get others to give you a chance to speak?
   - What can you do if a team member talks too much?

Sharing in a game: Ask students to name their favorite games at recess. Pick one game that has two sides, such as softball, and put the following list on the board. Discuss each step.
   - Agree on the rules. *Why is this important? Why do we have rules?*
   - Choose sides. *Describe how to choose sides without hurting feelings. Why is this important?*
   - Select the side who starts. *Is there a fair way to do this that will avoid problems?*

SHARING

- Wait for your turn. *How is this sharing? Why is it important?*
- *At the end of the game, what might the winners say to the losers? What might the losers say to the winners?*

Sharing talents: To demonstrate that "the whole is greater than the sum of its parts," have the class make a cooperative picture. Working in groups of 4, each student has a piece of paper. Pick one topic or subject to draw. Tell class what to draw on the paper, one part at a time. After each step, the student passes his paper to the next person and receives another. Thus, each picture in the group will have 4 different artists. Examples of topics and steps:

Person	Garden	Face
head	flowers	shape of face
body	different flowers	eyes, mouth
arms, legs	an insect	nose, ears
clothes	a surprise in garden	hair

Helping hand: *One way to share is to help someone else. You are sharing your time, your talents, or skills when you help someone pick up crayons they've dropped or you read a story to a younger student. Let's brainstorm a list of all the ways you can help each other. How can you "lend a hand?"*

Have each student draw an outline of his hand, cut it out, and tape it to his desk. Every time students "lend a hand," have them reward themselves by putting a star on the hand.

Sharing can be problem solving: If students don't already know how to fill out a problem-solving chart, teach them the format. (See unit for problem solving.) Give them problems they might encounter where sharing would be a good solution. Problems might be:
- You want to play on the bars but someone else is on them.
- You want to go to the listening center, but someone is there.
- You want to play with the truck, but someone has it already.

My problem is:

Choices (things to try)	Consequences Good	Not so good
1.	1.	1.
2.	2.	2.
3.	3.	3.

My best choice might be:

QUOTATIONS

Kindness in words creates confidence.
Kindness in giving creates love. (Lao-tzu)

Three helping one another will do as much as six men singly.
(Spanish proverb)

It is not what you give your friend, but what you are willing to give
him, that determines the quality of friendship. (Mary Dixon Thayer)

He who gives to me teaches me to give. (Danish proverb)

We must not only give what we have, we must also give what we
are.

Your luck is how you treat people.

Friends are made by many acts -- and lost by only one.

Be what you wish others to become.

For it is in giving that we receive. (St. Francis of Assisi)

The manner of giving is worth more than the gift. (Pierre Cornelle)

The more he gives to others, the more he possesses of his own.
(Lao-tzu)

SHARING

Friends share all things. (Pythagoras)

No act of kindness, no matter how small, is ever wasted. (Aesop)

Have you had a kindness shown? Pass it on. (Henry Burton)

What goes around, comes around.

When we are truly giving to others, we do so without expecting a reward in return.

GOAL CARDS

In addition to the "Lend a hand" practice activity, use other goal cards to recognize sharing. Examples of goal cards measuring this skill: "The best vitamin for making friends: B-1," "Watch my garden grow when I share," and "Pay yourself 1¢."

HOMEWORK COUPONS

Send home coupons to practice sharing at home during the month you work on this unit.

Social Skill: Sharing   **Month:**

Monday	Tuesday	Wednesday	Thursday	Friday
Introduction Set: Literature: T-chart:	Motto/Quote/ Song:	Class Meeting:	Sponge:	Class Meeting:
Practice:	Sponge:	Class Meeting:	Sponge:	Class Meeting:
Practice:	Sponge:	Class Meeting:	Sponge:	Class Meeting:
Practice:	Sponge:	Class Meeting:	Sponge:	Class Meeting:

RECOGNIZING FEELINGS

Social skill book: *Finding Feelings*

DIRECTIONS

Plan approximately one month for this unit. On Day 1, introduce the skill, read the social skill book, and fill in a T-chart with the class. For the remainder of the month, take 5 to 10 minutes a day for practice or sponge activities.

INTRODUCE SOCIAL SKILL TO CLASS

Be good detectives, using both your eyes and ears, to see if you can tell how I'm feeling. Role play happy, sad, angry, and afraid. *What clues did you use to tell how I was feeling?*

SOCIAL SKILL BOOK

Show cover of book to class. *How are Kittone, the kitty, and Mikelle feeling right now? How do you know? The title is "Finding Feelings." What do you think the book might be about?* Read the book. Ask the story comprehension questions of the first page.

ADDITIONAL LITERATURE SELECTIONS

Aliki. *Feelings*
Behrens, J. *How I Feel*
Bennett, W. *The Book of Virtues:*
    p. 110: Little Sunshine
    p. 143: Grandmother's Table
    p. 443: Chicken Little
    p. 445: The Wee-Wee Woman
Berman, C. *What Am I Doing in a Step-Family?*
Blume, J. *The Pain and the Great One*
Blume, J. *Otherwise Known As Sheila the Great*
DeClements, B. *Nothing's Fair in Fifth Grade*
Hogan, P. & K. Hogan. *The Hospital Scares Me*
Polacco, P. *Thunder Cake*

Viorst, J. *My Mama Says There Aren't Any Zombies, Ghosts, Vampires, Creatures, Demons, Monsters, Fiends, Goblins, or Things.*
Williams, M. *The Velveteen Rabbit*

T-CHART

Fill in a T-chart for each feeling, perhaps one a day. For each feeling, ask what the clues are from a person's body and face (looks like) and from what a person says (sounds like) to find out how they are feeling.

Happy

Looks like	Sounds like
smiling	pleasant voice
mouth is open	kind words
excited	laughing

Sad

Looks like	Sounds like
head down	maybe crying
little frown	quiet, soft voice
shoulders down, slumped	sniffing
looking down	
little or no eye contract	

Mad / Angry

Looks like	Sounds like
mouth/eyes frowning	yelling
eyes frowning (slanted eyebrow)	loud voice
clenched fists	bad words
wrinkles on forehead	loud voice
arms crossed	"That makes me mad."
unfriendly	"I've had it."
glaring	"You're terrible."

Afraid

Looks like	Sounds like
wide eyes	"Help!"
mouth open	a scream
shaking	"Oh, no!"

Hurt Feelings

Looks like	Sounds like
small frown	crying
head down	sniffing
little or no eye contact	"Nobody likes me."
looking down	"I don't have any friends."
blank look	"What'd I do wrong?"

PRACTICE ACTIVITIES

Collages: Using old magazines, partners cut out faces that show the feelings you have been studying. After demonstrating how to make a collage, let each partnership categorize and paste their own collage. Either hang as mobiles or create a bulletin board display, placing pictures around the poem, *Finding Feelings,* found on last page of social skill book.

Categorizing feelings: Using old magazines, partners cut out faces that express the feelings they have been studying. Create a large classroom chart from butcher paper and let them glue their contributions in the correct columns. When complete, discuss with the class the similarities of facial expressions within each column.

Happy	Sad	Hurt Feelings	Angry	Afraid

Feelings strips: Give each student a strip of paper with the five faces printed on it. (Permission is granted to copy model on first page of social skill book, *Finding Feelings*.) Describe a situation, ask students to point to the feeling they might have in that situation. Let partners share their answers with each other. Examples of situations might be:

- Your friend didn't invite you to his birthday party.
- You asked a friend to play and he said "No."
- You asked a friend to play and he said "Yes."
- A bully said he was going to beat you up after school.
- Your teacher said you do great work in class.
- Another student tore the picture you drew.
- You forgot to bring your lunch to school.
- A group of kids were teasing you at recess.
- While you're playing softball, the kids aren't playing fair.

Feeling words: Take one feeling at a time and brainstorm words associated with that feeling. This activity can be done (a) as a whole group discussion activity, (b) by small cooperative groups, or (c) as a categorizing activity when you give the words out of order and students rewrite them into appropriate feeling categories.

Happy: glad, delighted, excited, joyous, enjoying, ecstatic, cheerful, pleased, bubbly, elated, overjoyed, radiant, jubilant, gay, gleeful, merry, sunny, festive
Sad: disappointed, unhappy, depressed, sorrowful, miserable, blue, gloomy, forlorn, dejected, defeated, burdened, crushed
Hurt feelings: insulted, teased, called names, feeling pain, grief, deep sorrow, crushed, tormented, rejected, heartbroken
Angry: mad, furious, annoyed, irritated, hostile, bitter, fuming, boiling, hateful, offensive, enraged, cross, provoked
Afraid: fearful, frightened, scared, full of fear, terrified, panicked, nervous, shaky, threatened, alarmed, quaking

Additional vocabulary: depressed, disgusted, confident, embarrassed, cautious, overwhelmed, jealous, shocked, exhausted, guilty, suspicious, understanding, optimistic, considerate, affectionate, tenacious, dynamic, fascinated, intrigued, engrossed, curious, impulsive, frisky

Alphabet book: When students are acquainted with feeling vocabulary, have them write an alphabet book of feelings they've had, describing and illustrating each entry. (A = angry, B = bored, C = crushed....)

Role play: Write the following situations on cards. A student draws a card, reads it to the class, and must role play the situation. The class must guess which feeling he is showing.

- You got lost on the way home from a friend's house.
- Your kite is stuck in a tree.
- Big kids are calling you names on the playground.
- You won a prize in a contest for a story you wrote.
- Your mom says you're moving to a new school.
- You don't get to watch your favorite TV program.
- A kid says your coloring is ugly.
- The teacher says you are a good reader.

Different feelings:

Sometimes the same situation may cause different feelings in people. How many of you are afraid of a snake? Not all of you will have the same feeling.

How many of you are happy when we get to stay inside for a rainy day recess? How many of you are sad because you wish you could play outdoors?

Give the class the following list. Each child should write the feeling that each situation would cause. (Young children could draw the face.) Let partners compare their answers.

- It's Halloween. You get to visit a haunted house.
- It's your turn to go down the giant water slide at the swimming pool.
- You didn't get your schoolwork done so you can't go out to recess.
- You can't find the toy you wanted to play with.
- Your family says you are moving to a new city.

Changing feelings: *Sometimes our feelings change as we change and grow. How many of you were afraid to come to school on the first day of Kindergarten? How many of you are afraid now? Let's brainstorm a list of things you used to be afraid of but aren't afraid of now. Examples might be going to the doctor, turning off the lights at bedtime, going out to recess, or riding a bike.*

Now let's brainstorm a list of times you felt sad about something, but no longer feel sad. Examples might be having to change classrooms at the end of the school year, moving to a new house, or your best friend moves away.

Predicting feelings: Students need to be able to predict the feelings of others, particularly how their actions cause those feelings. First, play the koosh ball game by describing a situation (cause), then throwing the ball to a student to predict the feeling (effect).

- If the teacher gives Abby a hug, Abby might feel....
- If Ben lost his favorite coat, he might feel....
- If Carla heard kids telling lies about her, she might feel....
- If Gloria's mom made her go to bed early for being rude, Gloria might feel....
- If Jay shares his candy bar with Jenny, she might feel....
- If Sue took Will's crayon box without asking, he might feel....

Next, have students sit with their partner to describe their feelings to each other.

- If I didn't give my partner a chance to talk, my partner would feel....
- If I asked my partner for her opinion, she would feel....
- If I boss my partner around, he would feel....
- If I didn't listen to my partner, she would feel....
- If I told my partner he draws well, he would feel....
- If I copied my partner's work, she would feel....
- If I didn't share with my partner, he would feel....
- If I said, "Nice job." to my partner, she would feel....

Poetry: Provide poems for students to interpret. For example, ask students to rewrite the following Emily Dickinson poem in their own words.

If I can stop one heart from breaking,
I shall not live in vain;
If I can ease one life the aching,
Or cool one pain,
Or help one fainting robin
Unto his nest again,
I shall not live in vain.

SPONGES

My mom would say I'm happiest when....
My saddest moment was when....
My family would say I'm angriest when....
I get mad at school when....
My feelings are hurt at school when....
My feelings are hurt at home when....

FEELINGS

The time I was most scared was when....
When it's my turn to talk and my classmates aren't listening, I feel....
If a little girl was lost at the zoo, she might feel ... because....
My best friend is sad when....
At school, I am happiest when....
I am a person who
       is happy when....
       is sad when....
       has hurt feelings when....
       is angry when....
       is afraid of....

QUOTATIONS

True happiness (if understood)
Consists alone in doing good. (Thomson)

Mankind has become so much one family that we cannot insure our own prosperity except by insuring that of everyone else. If you wish to be happy yourself, you must resign yourself to seeing others also happy. (Bertrand Russell)

Whoever is happy will make others happy, too. He who has courage and faith will never perish in misery! (Anne Frank)

Very little is needed to make a happy life. (Marcus Aurelius)

The time to be happy is now.
The place to be happy is here.
The way to be happy is to make others so. (Robt. Green Ingersoll)

If you want to be happy, be. (Alexei Tolstoi)

Happiness is a warm puppy. (Charles Schultz)

We hold these truths to be self-evident; that all men are created equal; that they are endowed by their creator with certain unalienable rights; that among these are life, liberty, and the pursuit of happiness. (Thomas Jefferson, Declaration of Independence)

Speak when you're angry--and you'll make the best speech you'll ever regret. (Henry Ward Beecher)

Anger manages everything badly. (Latin proverb)

When a man is wrong and won't admit it, he always gets angry.
(Haliburton)

If anger is not restrained, it is frequently more hurtful to us than the
injury that provokes it. (Seneca)

When anger rises, think of the consequences. Be master of thine
anger. (Confucius)

The worst thing that happens to a man may be the best thing that
ever happened to him if he doesn't let it get the best of him.

Sometimes the best gain is to lose.

The diamond cannot be polished with friction, nor man perfected
without trials.

Trying times are times for trying.

Trouble is only opportunity in work clothes.

Only one person in the whole wide world can defeat you. That is
yourself!

The difference between stumbling blocks and stepping stones is the
way a man uses them.

He who has learned to disagree without being disagreeable has
discovered the most valuable secret of a diplomat.

Wise men are not always silent, but know when to be.

If you are patient in one moment of anger, you will escape a hundred
days of sorrow. (Chinese proverb)

Anger is not only inevitable, it is necessary. Its absence means
indifference, the most disastrous of all human failings.
(Arthur Ponsonby)

We choose our joys and sorrows long before we experience them.

FEELINGS

Use disappointment as material for patience.

Oh, a trouble's a ton, or a trouble's an ounce,
Or a trouble is what you make it.
And it isn't the fact that you're hurt that counts,
But only how did you take it. (Edmund Cooke)

Learn from the mistakes of others--you can't live long enough to make them all yourself.

One learns manners from those who have none.

He who fears something gives it power over him. (Moorish proverb)

GOAL CARDS

Use goal cards for measuring success both for recognizing feelings and recognizing the cause-and-effect nature of feelings. For example, young children could draw a face that shows each feeling they recognize. To promote empathy, have students give themselves a point every time they can tell why someone had a particular feeling. For example:
He was sad because his dog ran away.
She was afraid because the dog was growling at her.

HOMEWORK COUPONS

Send home one coupon every few days to promote transfer of training.

Monday	Tuesday	Wednesday	Thursday	Friday
Introduction Set: Literature: T-chart:	Motto/Quote/Song:	Class Meeting:	Sponge:	Class Meeting:
Practice:	Sponge:	Class Meeting:	Sponge:	Class Meeting:
Practice:	Sponge:	Class Meeting:	Sponge:	Class Meeting:
Practice:	Sponge:	Class Meeting:	Sponge:	Class Meeting:

TATTLING VS. REPORTING

Social skill book: *Tattlin' Madeline*

DIRECTIONS

Plan approximately one month for the unit. On Day 1, introduce the skill, read the social skill book, and construct a T-chart with the class. For the remainder of the month, take 5 to10 minutes a day for at least one practice activity or sponge. This unit is most effective when it follows the unit on problem solving. Deciding what to report and what can be handled alone is a type of problem solving. Fill in the monthly calendar with the activities you select.

INTRODUCE THE SOCIAL SKILL TO CLASS

What do you know about tattletales? Have you ever called someone a tattletale? Why? Would you want to be called a tattletale?

SOCIAL SKILL BOOK

Let's predict what this book is going to be about just from the title. What can you tell from the picture of Madeline? Read the book. Ask the story comprehension questions included on the first page.

ADDITIONAL LITERATURE SELECTIONS

Silverstein, S. *Falling Up:*
p. 9: *Complainin' Jack*

T-CHART

Let's fill out a T-chart for reporters, then fill out a T-chart for tattletales.

Reporter

Looks like	Sounds like
worried	"Someone is going to be hurt."
concerned	"John needs help right away."
trying to help	"May I help you?"
thinking before acting	"I tried to help but couldn't, so I'm reporting this to you."
	"I saw a dangerous weapon on the playground."

Tattletale

Looks like	Sounds like
pointing finger at someone else	"Teacher, she took my paper."
not helping others with problem	whining
angry, fists clenched	yelling

T-signal: *Sometimes when you come up to me to tell me something, I will make the "T" sign with my hands, like the teacher did in the book, Tattlin' Madeline. When I do, I want you to think about why you are telling me. If someone is going to be hurt or if property is going to be damaged, tell me. For example, say "I am telling you because someone is going to be hurt." But, if after thinking about why you are telling me you decide you're tattling, say "Sorry" and walk away.*

SPONGES

I don't want to be a tattletale because....
A problem I handled by myself was....
A problem I shouldn't handle by myself would be....
An example of tattling would be when....
An example of reporting would be when....
If someone called my best friend a name, I would....
If someone didn't give me a turn at tetherball, I would....

If my friend left his coat out on the playground, I would....
If I saw a boy climbing the school roof to get a ball, I would....

PRACTICE ACTIVITIES

Instead of tattling: Make a list of the many things students have told you previously that fit into the category "tattling" and could have been handled by the student first. Examples might be:
- That boy took my pencil.
- That kid is looking at my paper.
- They're making faces at me.
- I had the ball first and she took it from me.
- He won't give me a turn at the computer.

With students working in pairs, have them brainstorm 2 or 3 ways they could solve the problem without telling the teacher. Taking one problem at a time, have students role play their solutions.

What would happen if... Give students practice in recognizing why certain problems should be reported to an adult. *We're going to play a game called "What would happen if...." and you must predict what might happen.* After the predictions are made, ask students if they should report this problem to an adult and why. Help them label if property might be damaged or a person hurt.
- Someone brought a knife to school.
- You saw a girl set off the school fire alarm.
- You saw a fifth grader steal lunch money.

What do you do next? *Even the very best problem solvers can't solve all of their problems. Sometimes you'll decide to handle a problem yourself, but your solution doesn't work. You have to decide what to do next. I'll give you a problem and a solution that didn't work. You and your partner figure out what you'd do next.*
- A boy knocked books off a desk. You asked him to pick them up and he said no. Now what?
- Another student was copying your work. You asked her not to, but she's still copying it.

QUOTATIONS

One reason why a dog is such a lovable creature is that his tail wags instead of his tongue.

Nobody raises his reputation by lowering others'.

The man who deals in sunshine is the man who wins the crowds.
He does a lot more business than the man who peddles clouds.

Before you flare up at any one's faults, take time to count to ten--ten
of your own.

Fault finders never improve the world; they only make it seem
worse than it really is.

Tact is the ability to close your mouth before someone else wants to.

Try to fix the mistake--never the blame.

If you want to put the world right, start with yourself.

Wise men are not always silent, but know when to be.

Be sure your brain is in gear before engaging your mouth.

GOAL CARDS

This is a difficult skill to record on a goal card because you
want students to report when necessary. The easiest way of
recording the use of the skill is to list those problems that were
solved by the student and those that needed to be reported.

Problems I solved myself	Problems I reported
1.	1.
2.	2.
3.	3.

HOMEWORK COUPONS

The ability to discriminate tattling from reporting is easier to
transfer when a child has brothers or sisters at home. However, give
all students a chance to take coupons home to encourage them to
discuss the difference with family members.

SOCIAL SKILL: TATTLING VS. REPORTING   MONTH:

Monday	Tuesday	Wednesday	Thursday	Friday
Introduction Set: Literature: T-chart:	Motto/Quote/Song:	Class Meeting:	Sponge:	Class Meeting:
Practice:	Sponge:	Class Meeting:	Sponge:	Class Meeting:
Practice:	Sponge:	Class Meeting:	Sponge:	Class Meeting:
Practice:	Sponge:	Class Meeting:	Sponge:	Class Meeting:

THE "T-SIGN"

TATTLING VS. REPORTING

MANNERS

Social skill book: *Copy the Cat*

DIRECTIONS

Plan approximately one month for the unit. On Day 1, introduce the skill, read the social skill book, and make a T-chart with the class. For the remainder of the month, take 5 to 10 minutes a day for at least one practice activity or sponge. Make every attempt to integrate manners with your existing content instruction.

INTRODUCE THE SOCIAL SKILL TO CLASS

If your best friend has good manners, what special words might you hear your best friend say when you share something with him? When your best friend wants to join in a game with you? When your best friend accidentally bumps into you? What do we call people who don't have good manners? (rude)

SOCIAL SKILL BOOK

Let's predict what this story is going to be about. Who are the characters? What can you tell about the book from the title? Ask the story comprehension questions on page 1 as you read.

ADDITIONAL LITERATURE SELECTIONS

Bennett, W. *The Book of Virtues*
    p. 24: Please
    p. 74: George Washington's Rules of Civility
    p. 171: Count That Day Lost
Bennett, W. *The Moral Compass*
    p. 159: Rules of Behavior
Silverstein, S. *A Light in the Attic*
    p. 132: Friendship
    p. 135: Hinges
    p. 148: Ladies First
Wells, R. *Timothy Goes to School*

T-CHART

Which character in the story had good manners? Who was rude? Let's write down what Sir Walter did and said that showed good manners. Then, let's write down what Copy did and said when he was rude.

Good Manners

Looks like	Sounds like
helping someone carry a big load	"Please"
sharing your snack	"Thank you"
a nod and a smile	"Excuse me"
holding the door open for someone whose arms are full	"May I please..."
writing a thank you note when you receive a gift or something special is done for you	"How are you?"

Rude

Looks Like	Sounds like
pushing	whining
fidgeting	contradicting
fussing around	nagging
acting like a nuisance	bragging/boasting
writing notes while someone is talking to you	whispering while someone is talking to you

SPONGES

You would be my best friend if....
You would be my worst enemy if....
List times when you've shown good manners.
Brainstorm ways to practice good manners with a new student in class.
List ways you could show good manners to a guest teacher (substitute).
How did you feel when someone was rude to you?
Brainstorm all the words you can think of to describe a rude person.
If a student trips on her way to the chalkboard, I would....
If a person singing in front of the class hit a bad note, I would....

PRACTICE ACTIVITIES

Emily Post (1922) said etiquette "...is to make the world a pleasanter place to live in, and you a more pleasant person to live with." Elizabeth Post (1984) described etiquette as "...a code of behavior, based on kindness and consideration." Manners are the tools that help us live by that code. The guiding principle for manners is thoughtfulness. Keep in mind that what is considered good manners and thoughtfulness is ever changing. The following activities are subject to such change!

Word Sort: Put the following terms/phrases on word cards. Let students arrange them into two columns and then name each column. (Or, put the list on the overhead projector and let students write them as two columns.)

good sport	bossy	pushy	takes your ball
trustworthy	tells secrets	loyal	polite
tattles to teacher	wrecks your game	tries to be center of attention	talks out of turn in class
doesn't share	kind	dependable	teases
helpful	puts others down	fighter	cooperative

"Wanted Poster": Working in cooperative groups, ask students to brainstorm what they would want in a friend (use Roundtable). Have them take their ideas and create a "Wanted" poster: "Wanted, a friend who...."

Acrostics: Groups can pick their word and design an acrostic for the word.

F	P	M	R
R	O	A	U
I	L	N	D
E	I	N	E
N	T	E	
D	E	R	
S		S	

An example:

   May I please....
   Allow me to help you....
   Now it's your turn.
   No, thank you.
   Excuse me.
   Remember to say....
   Sorry.

Situational manners: Use the cooperative structure, "Corners", by posting a different situation in each corner of the room.   Students pick a corner to chart what good manners would look like in each case.

   • You have 3 cookies and you are playing with four friends.
   • Two students are playing a computer game and you want to join them.
   • The teacher is talking to someone else and you want to interrupt.
   • You bring a new friend home after school.

Or, make the situations generic:

   • In the lunchroom (or, while eating)
   • On the playground
   • At a movie
   • During an assembly
   • In traffic
   • On a bus
   • In the classroom

Situation Web: Have students develop a web.   Fill in what it would sound like using manners in these situations.   This is also an opportunity to integrate the skill of using quotation marks.

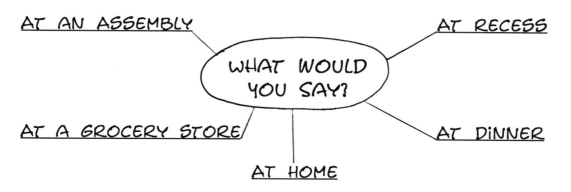

Rude Dude vs. Polite Knight: Have students create flip books contrasting a rude dude with a polite knight. (Or, title the book: "From Rudeville to Point Polite")

Provide situations when someone:
- falls off a skate board
- forgets a pencil
- is all alone at recess
- bumps into you
- accidentally takes your pencil

Manners Rap, written by Joe Kollner, Cincinnati, Ohio

We use manners, we use them every day.
They make you feel good in every way.
Words like please and may I, too,
You're welcome, excuse me, and thank you.

Treat other people in a way that's kind.
Do it every day and soon you'll find
You have lots of friends. People like you.
Better than that, you'll like yourself, too.

Life is too short for arguments and fights.
Remember your manners, respect human rights.
Don't act mean or keep your fingers curled.
Use your manners, create a better world.

So respect each other, listen to your heart.
In our room, manners play a part.

QUOTATIONS

Kindness given is never lost.
The test of good manners is being able to put up pleasantly with bad ones.
Who gossips to you will gossip of you.
The secret of patience is doing something else in the meantime.
Friends are made by many acts and lost by only one.
The greater the man, the greater the courtesy.

Put yourself in his place.

What counts is not the number of hours you put in, but how much you put in the hours.

Never miss an opportunity to make others happy, even if you have to let them alone to do it.

One great use of words is to hide our thoughts.

Manners are the happy way of doing things.

The way to be happy is to make others happy. Helping others is the secret of all success – in business, in the arts, and in the home.

Happiness is not a station you arrive at, but a manner of traveling.

Tact is the art of making a point without making an enemy. (Newton)

The thoughtless are rarely wordless. (Newton)

The kindly word that falls today may bear its fruit tomorrow.

A good manner springs from a good heart and fine manners are the outcome of unselfish kindness.

A gentleman is a gentle man.

Fault finders never improve the world. They only make it seem worse than it really is.

One learns manners from those who have none.

We have committed the Golden Rule to memory; now let us commit it to life.

There was a gentle whisper, toss, and wiggle
But etiquette forbade them all to giggle.   (Byron)

Proverbs

A clear conscience is a good pillow.

A closed mouth catcheth no flies.

A word and a stone once let go cannot be recalled.

Always taking out and never putting in soon reaches the bottom.

Beauty without virtue is like a rose without scent.

Virtue is its own reward.

A kind word is like a spring day. (Russian)

By a sweet tongue and kindness, you can drag an elephant with a hair. (Persian)

None is so rich as to throw away a friend. (Turkish)

A friend is a poem. (Persian)

He who seeks a faultless friend, remains friendless. (Turkish)

When men are friendly, even water is sweet. (Chinese)

Virtue and politeness are inseparable. (Confucius)

Monday	Tuesday	Wednesday	Thursday	Friday
Introduction Set: Literature: T-chart:	Motto/Quote/ Song:	Class Meeting:	Sponge:	Class Meeting:
Practice:	Sponge:	Class Meeting:	Sponge:	Class Meeting:
Practice:	Sponge:	Class Meeting:	Sponge:	Class Meeting:
Practice:	Sponge:	Class Meeting:	Sponge:	Class Meeting:

REPRODUCIBLES

• The owner of this guidebook grants permission to reproduce the following forms for classroom use only.

• It is suggested that you make a single copy of each of the following pages to use as a master for all future copies. That will preserve the book pages as a backup. No page numbers are printed on the forms.

• In an effort to conserve paper, the coupons, template, and goal cards are designed to fit four forms per page. The generic homework form and letter to parents allow for two forms per page. Small guiding marks indicate where to cut.

• Included in this section are:

1. Goal cards
   Copy on brightly colored, lightweight tag.

2. A template for problem solving
   This can be made into small notebook pads for students to use at their desks for their own problem solving. It also serves as an action plan for students who have misbehaved in class and need to consider their other choices.

3. Letter to parents
   This letter explains the use of the homework coupons you may be sending home with students. This, or a similar letter, should be sent home with the first homework coupon.

4. Homework coupons
   The first example is a generic homework form that could be used with any of the social skills. The remaining coupons are specific to the skill identified on each.

Name:

My T-chart for the skill:

Looks like	Sounds like

I want to try this skill with:

This is what happened when I tried the skill:

······················   ·················

Name:

My T-chart for the skill:

Looks like	Sounds like

I want to try this skill with:

This is what happened when I tried the skill:

Inching along

It is only through change that we grow.

Reach for
the stars.

Going in the right direction.

Name _____

Name _____

	Gave put-up	Shared	Listened
Monday			
Tuesday			
Wednesday			
Thursday			
Friday			

Pay yourself 1¢
each time you use the skill.

PAYDAY!   I EARNED _____

We shared.	YES NO
We gave a put-up.	YES NO
We used eye contact	YES NO
We stayed calm.	YES NO
We gave ideas.	YES NO
We _____	YES!

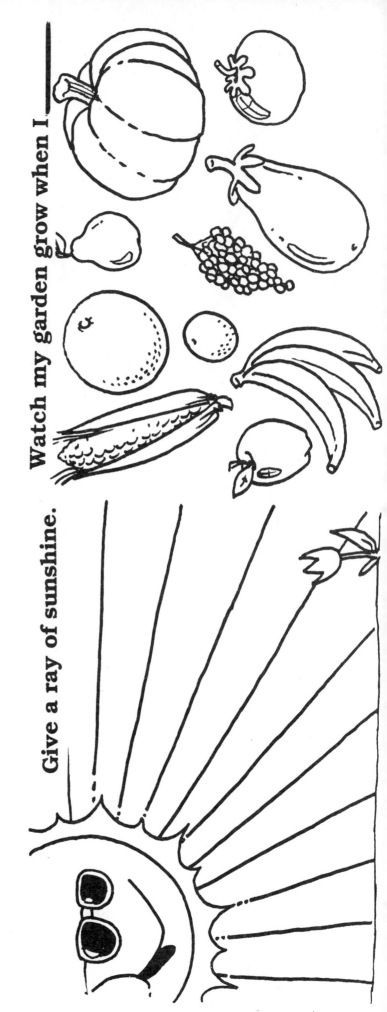

Watch my garden grow when I _____

Give a ray of sunshine.

PUT-UP SCOREBOARD

HOME
(GAVE ONE)

VISITORS
(GOT ONE)

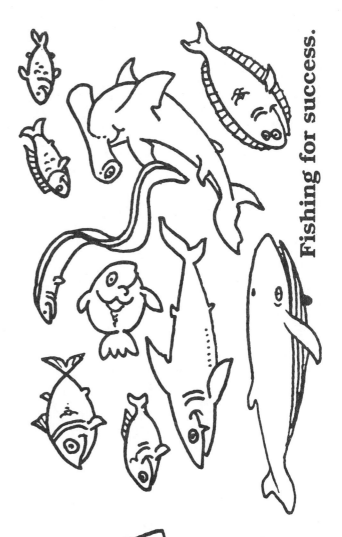

Fishing for success.

One thing you can't recycle is time.

The best vitamin for making friends: B-1.

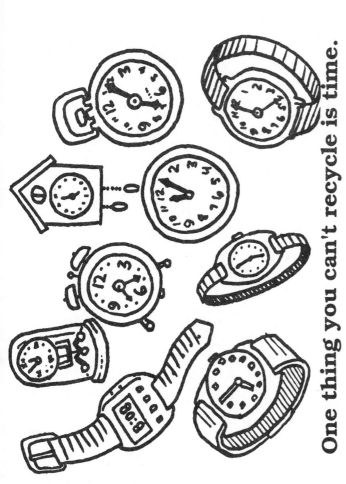

Kick your year off with good manners.

Please.　　Excuse me.　　Thank you.　　May I...

You're welcome.　Good morning.　I'm sorry.

Would you like to play?　Please, may I use...

Tune in to

Light up our lives with put-ups.

Flying high above the crowd.

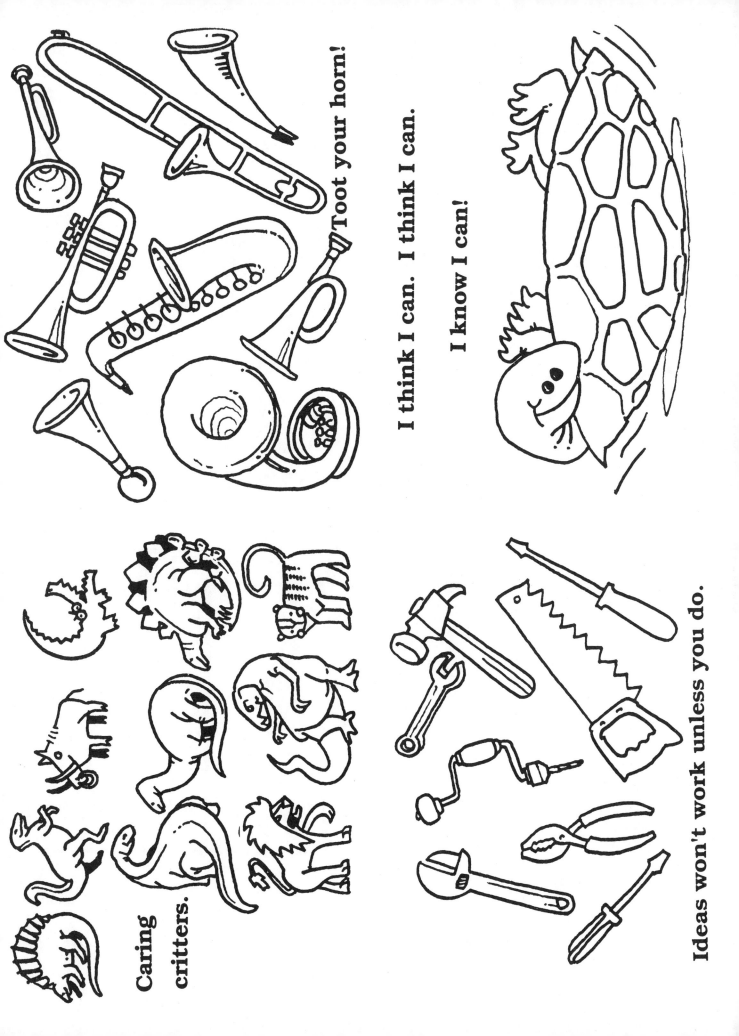

Toot your horn!

I think I can. I think I can.

I know I can!

Caring critters.

Ideas won't work unless you do.

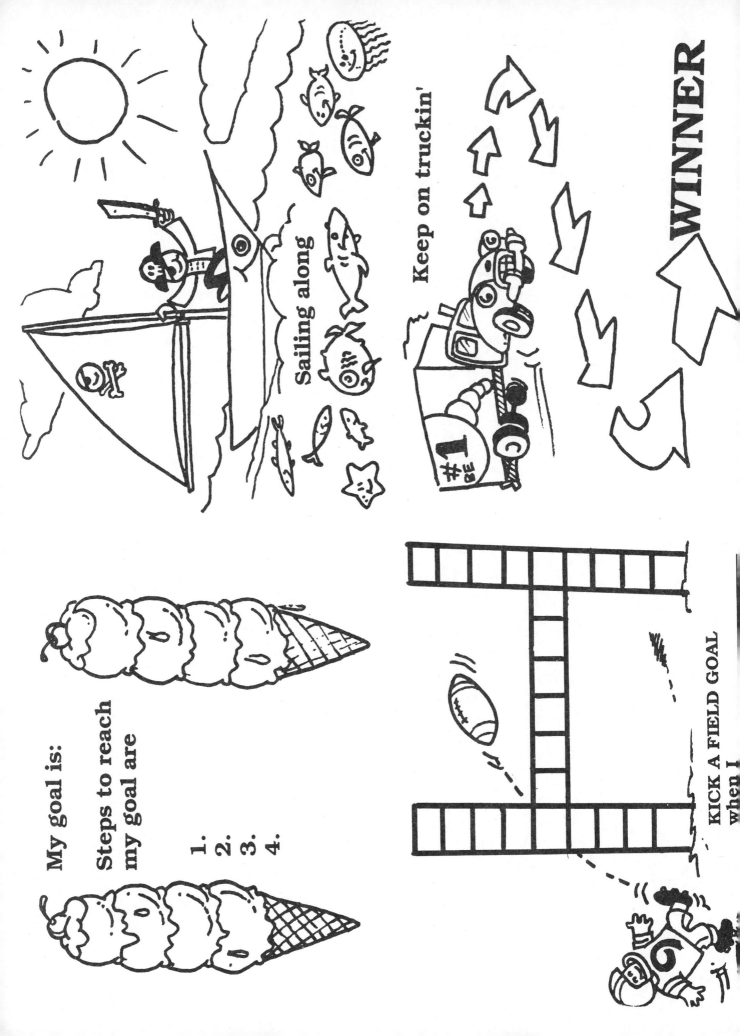

Sailing along

Keep on truckin'

BE #1

WINNER

My goal is:

Steps to reach
my goal are

1.
2.
3.
4.

KICK A FIELD GOAL
when I

My Problem:

Choices (things to try)	Consequences	
	Why?	Why not?
1.	1.	1.
2.	2.	2.
3.	3.	3.
4	4.	4.

My best solution is:

My Problem:

Choices (things to try)	Consequences	
	Why?	Why not?
1.	1.	1.
2.	2.	2.
3.	3.	3.
4	4.	4.

My best solution is:

Dear Families:

One of our school goals is to help children get along with others. In fact, we have a section of our report card grading a child's ability to get along with others in class.

In class we will be working on the social skills of listening, giving compliments, taking turns, problem solving, and dealing with anger. Because we want your child to practice these skills at home, we will be sending homework coupons. Please fill out the coupons with your child, sign the homework, and return it the next day.

Thank you for your help.

Sincerely,

Homework for LISTENING

When I listen, this is what I look like:

When I listen, this is what I sound like:

Family member signature _____

Homework for LISTENING

These are the people who listened to me today:

Family member signature _____

Homework for LISTENING

These are the times I listened today:

Family member signature _____

Homework for LISTENING

It is important to listen because:

Family member signature _____

Homework for PROBLEM SOLVING

I had a problem when:

I solved it by:

Family member signature _____

Homework for PROBLEM SOLVING

My problem:

My choices to solve this problem are:
1.
2.
3.

The consequences of these choices would be:
1.
2.
3.

The best solution is:

Family member signature _____

Homework for PROBLEM SOLVING

Here are problems I have solved by myself:

Here's a problem I couldn't solve by myself:

Family member signature

Homework for PROBLEM SOLVING

I want to be a good problem solver because:

This is what I would think about when I try to solve a problem:

Family member signature _____

Homework for PUT-UPS

When I get a put-up, I feel:

When I give a put-up, I feel:

Family member signature

Homework for PUT-UPS

Here is a list of put-ups I could give myself:

Family member signature

Homework for PUT-UPS

Today I gave a put-up to:

I said:

They said:

Family member signature

Homework for PUT-UPS

Here is a list of put-ups I could give my family:

Family member signature

Homework for DEALING WITH ANGER

These are things that make me mad:

It doesn't pay to lose my temper because:

Family member signature _____

Homework for DEALING WITH ANGER

Anger looks like:

Anger sounds like:

Calm looks like:

Calm sounds like:

Family member signature _____

Homework for DEALING WITH ANGER

I feel mad or angry when:

This is what I will try to do when I'm angry:

Family member signature _____

Homework for DEALING WITH ANGER

It makes me mad when someone:

The best way for me to deal with my anger is:

Family member signature _____

Homework for SHARING

These are the things I can share:

Family member signature _____

Homework for SHARING

At school I shared:

At home I shared:

Family member signature _____

Homework for SHARING

When I share, I feel:

When someone shares with me, I feel:

When my friends don't share, I feel:

Family member signature _____

Homework for SHARING

The people I shared with today are:

These people shared with me today:

Family member signature _____

Homework for FEELINGS

When a person is mad, he looks:

These are things that make a person feel angry:

Family member signature _____

Homework for FEELINGS

When a person is afraid, he looks:

These are the things that make a person feel afraid:

Family member signature _____

Homework for FEELINGS

When a person is happy, he looks:

These are things that make a person feel happy:

Family member signature _____

Homework for FEELINGS

When a person is sad, he looks:

These are the things that make a person feel sad:

Family member signature _____

Homework for REPORTING, NOT TATTLING

These are the kinds of things I would report:

These are problems I could solve or handle myself:

Family member signature _____

Homework for REPORTING, NOT TATTLING

These are the things I should always report to an adult:

Family member signature _____

Homework for REPORTING, NOT TATTLING

The reasons kids tattle are to:

I would report to an adult when:

Family member signature _____

Homework for REPORTING, NOT TATTLING

I would rather be a reporter than a tattletale because:

Family member signature _____

Homework for MANNERS

Here is a list of times at home when manners are important:

Family member signature_____

Homework for MANNERS

At the dinnertable, I would be rude if I:

Family member signature_____

Homework for MANNERS

Here are examples of manners I used at home last night:

Family member signature_____

Homework for MANNERS

Here are some of the things I can say on the telephone to be polite:

Family member signature_____